Date: 5/24/12

J 578.789 HEN
Henzel, Cynthia Kennedy,
Great Barrier Reef /

Troubled Treasures: World Heritage Sites

GREAT BARRIER REEF

Cynthia Kennedy Henzel

ABDO Publishing Company

visit us at
www.abdopublishing.com

Published by ABDO Publishing Company, 8000 West 78th Street, Edina, Minnesota 55439.
Copyright © 2011 by Abdo Consulting Group, Inc. International copyrights reserved in all
countries. No part of this book may be reproduced in any form without written permission from the
publisher. The Checkerboard Library™ is a trademark and logo of ABDO Publishing Company.

Printed in the United States of America, North Mankato, Minnesota.
102010
012011

Cover Photo: Fred Bavendam / Minden Pictures / National Geographic Stock
Interior Photos: Alamy pp. 12, 14, 15, 19; Corbis p. 25; Getty Images pp. 21, 23, 28–29;
    iStockphoto p. 4; Norbert Wu / Minden Pictures / National Geographic Stock p. 5;
    Peter Arnold pp. 1, 9, 17, 27; Photolibrary pp. 7, 9, 13, 18

Series Coordinator: BreAnn Rumsch
Editors: Megan M. Gunderson, BreAnn Rumsch
Art Direction & Cover Design: Neil Klinepier

Library of Congress Cataloging-in-Publication Data

Henzel, Cynthia Kennedy, 1954-
  Great Barrier Reef / Cynthia Kennedy Henzel.
     p. cm. -- (Troubled treasures : world heritage sites)
  Includes index.
  ISBN 978-1-61613-564-5
  1. Great Barrier Reef (Qld.)--Juvenile literature. 2. Coral reef ecology--Australia--Great Barrier
     Reef (Qld.)--Juvenile literature. I. Title.
  GB468.89.H46 2011
  551.42'409943--dc22
                              2010021310

CONTENTS

City in the Sea 4

The Stuff of Reefs 6

Building Blocks. 8

Discovering the Reef 10

Wildlife Wonderland 12

Human Influence. 16

The Global Threat 20

Protecting the Reef 24

Positive Changes 26

A Living Laboratory 28

Glossary 30

Saying It 31

Web Sites. 31

Index 32

Beneath the Pacific Ocean lies a huge structure that resembles a busy city. The structure's walls are made of reefs. Holes and cracks in the walls house millions of sea creatures. Night and day, the Great Barrier Reef (GBR) is a busy place.

Like a city, this place is not one solid structure. It is made up of nearly 3,000 individual reefs! There are also hundreds of islands.

The GBR lies off the coast of Queensland in northeastern Australia. It stretches from a point near Bundaberg, Queensland, to the Torres Strait. That is about 1,250 miles (2,000 km).

The reef lies between 10 and 100 miles (16 and 160 km) away from Australia's coast. At its widest point, it extends 45 miles (72 km) across!

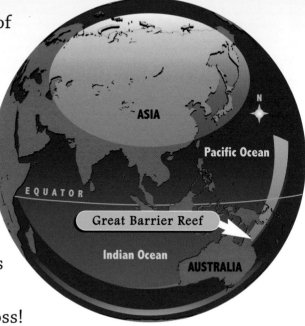

ASIA

N

Pacific Ocean

EQUATOR

Great Barrier Reef

Indian Ocean

AUSTRALIA

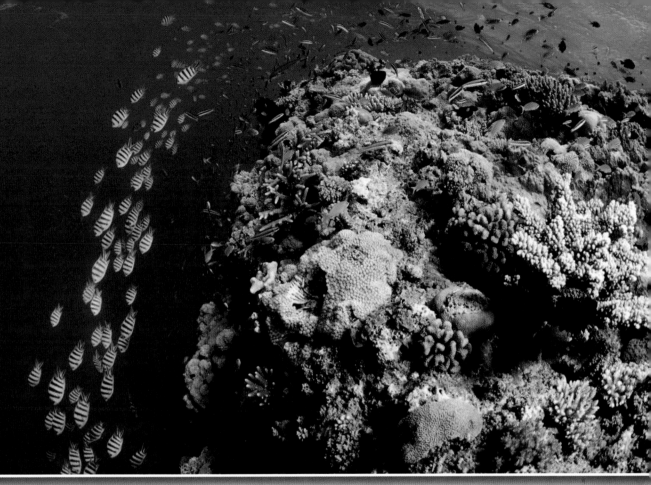

Much of the Great Barrier Reef lies in shallow water. The reef walls become steep where they meet the deep, open ocean.

The GBR is the largest reef system in the world. Its amazing plants and animals make it a natural treasure. **UNESCO** officials recognized the importance of the Great Barrier Reef by naming it a World Heritage site. That will help preserve this special place for years to come.

The GBR is the largest structure ever built by living organisms. Yet it was not made by humans. Creatures known as coral polyps formed it.

These animals are related to jellyfish and sea anemones. One end of a polyp's tiny, tubelike body attaches to a surface. At the other end, **tentacles** surround its mouth. These gather food.

Coral polyps form either hard or soft corals. When many polyps of the same type attach to one another they form a colony. Some colonies look like feathery fans. Others resemble plates, antlers, or brains.

Tiny algae called zooxanthellae live in the tissue of healthy polyps. Algae give many corals their color. When healthy, corals are usually green or brown. Without algae, most are white.

Polyps also get much of their food from the algae. The algae use the sun's energy to make food. So, most coral colonies grow in shallow water. There, the sun can reach the algae.

More to Explore
Soft coral polyps each have eight feathery tentacles.

Hard coral polyps have smooth tentacles that grow in groups of six.

Both hard and soft coral polyps live in the GBR. However, hard corals are mainly responsible for forming the reef.

To form hard corals, polyps draw in specks of limestone from the water. This helps them build a hard outer skeleton. As coral colonies develop, their skeletons attach to one another. This creates the coral shapes we recognize.

When polyps die, they leave behind their skeletons. The colonies continue to build on these remains. This growth slowly forms a reef.

Over time, sand and mud fill holes in the structure. Materials from other animals drop there as well. Eventually, all this compresses into great limestone walls.

It took millions of corals many years to build the GBR. In the north, much of the base is about 18 million years old! Most of the GBR's recent structure formed within the last 6,000 years.

Corals form many interesting shapes! In fact, they are often named for these shapes. Can you guess which common name belongs to each of these hard corals?

- *brain coral*   - *staghorn coral*   - *table coral*

Answers: A) table coral B) brain coral C) staghorn coral

DISCOVERING THE REEF

People have lived near the GBR for thousands of years. Aborigines are the native people of Australia. Most likely, they were the first to discover the reef.

In 1522, the first European saw the GBR. He was Portuguese captain Cristóvão de Mendonça. Then in 1770, British captain James Cook led the first European exploration there. Cook and his crew charted much of the area.

Eventually, the GBR became a site of scientific interest. In 1842, geologist J. Beete Jukes arrived. He spent four years studying the area.

Then in 1928, Great Britain started the Great Barrier Reef Expedition. Charles Maurice Yonge led 12 other scientists to Australia. There, they conducted research for about one year.

Yonge studied reef construction and reef life. This research had not been done before. His work was a big step for marine science.

More to Explore
The Great Barrier Reef is the only living thing visible from space.

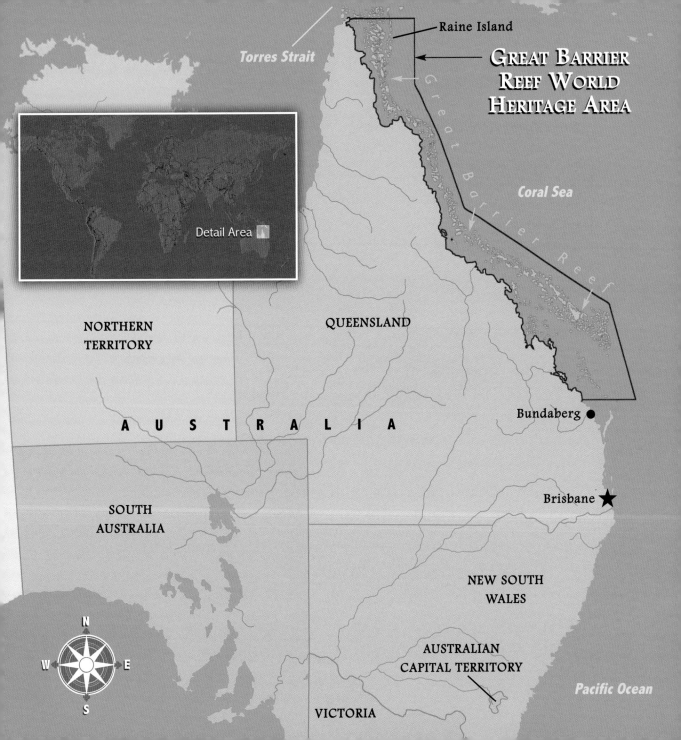

Torres Strait

Raine Island

GREAT BARRIER
REEF WORLD
HERITAGE AREA

Coral Sea

Great Barrier Reef

Detail Area

NORTHERN
TERRITORY

QUEENSLAND

A U S T R A L I A

Bundaberg ●

SOUTH
AUSTRALIA

Brisbane ★

NEW SOUTH
WALES

AUSTRALIAN
CAPITAL TERRITORY

N
W   E
S

S

VICTORIA

Pacific Ocean

Giant clams can grow more than three feet (1 m) long. They can weigh up to 500 pounds (230 kg)!

The Great Barrier Reef is full of amazing wildlife! About 1,500 species of fish call the reef home. That is more than any other marine **habitat**.

Marine mammals such as dolphins and whales can also be found there. Dugongs grow 7 to 11 feet (2 to 3 m) long and weigh 500 to 925 pounds (230 to 420 kg). These large, shy mammals can live for 73 years.

In this underwater wonderland, there are thousands of squid, octopuses, and shelled animals. Numerous giant clams live there. Some live up to 70 years.

Many smaller creatures can also be found in the GBR. These include shrimps, crabs, sea snakes, and starfish. And, there are about 1,500 types of sponges.

The most recognized residents are the corals. About 400 species live in the GBR. Even with such large numbers, these creatures still face danger.

A coral's most serious predator is the crown of thorns. This starfish can grow up to 18 inches (45 cm) across. Sometimes, large groups attack. They can destroy reefs by eating corals faster than they grow.

Chemicals from the crown of thorns's stomach slowly break down living polyps. The empty coral skeleton is left behind.

Mangrove roots provide good hiding and nesting places for small sea animals.

The Great Barrier Reef is more than an underwater wonderland. It also includes many islands. They are grouped into two types.

The larger islands are the tops of underwater mountains. The smaller islands formed from corals that grew above the water. Over time, waves broke down the corals into sand.

The islands provide homes and nesting sites for many animals. Six types of sea turtles are found among the islands. They commonly nest on Raine Island.

Hundreds of bird species live on the islands, too. These include pelicans, cormorants, and silver gulls. Boobies, tropical petrels, and other seabirds also visit.

Plants provide food and shelter for animals. Mangrove trees line many shores. Their roots grow down into the water and tangle beneath the surface. Underwater, beds of sea grass grow between the islands and throughout the GBR. Dugongs and other animals graze there.

The world's largest population of dugongs lives in the GBR.

HUMAN INFLUENCE

The GBR is home to countless plants and animals. These features attract many people. But, too many visitors can cause problems.

Tourism developed in the area in the 1980s. Many hotels were built along the reef. Even an airport was added. To make room for these structures, some natural landforms were destroyed.

Today, more than 2 million tourists visit every year. All these people put **stress** on the GBR. Visitors may frighten nesting animals. Careless swimmers and waders can easily break corals. Boats create noise and water pollution. The water can even become polluted from too much sunscreen!

Still, there are some simple ways to enjoy the GBR responsibly. For example, visitors should not litter on the reef. Garbage can harm all animals, including corals. People should also respect native species. This means moving carefully around corals and not touching or feeding other animals.

More to Explore
In the GBR, ten hard coral species are endemic. This means they are found nowhere else in the world.

Tourists use plastic viewers to see life underwater during reef walks.

Boats must carefully travel through narrow channels in the GBR.

Over the years, people have created **environmental** problems for the Great Barrier Reef. Oil spills and other accidents have occurred there. Fishing has lowered fish numbers. Nets harm animals, and boat anchors damage corals. These threats have upset the natural conditions of the water.

The way Australians use land can also cause serious problems. Agriculture and other industries add chemicals to the ground. These substances enter rivers and flow to the

From Queensland, 26 rivers flow into the reef. Cloudy swirls form where materials in the freshwater meet the ocean.

ocean. This changes the natural balance of the reef's ecosystem.

In addition, bits of dirt and other materials flow into the rivers. When it reaches the ocean, the water there becomes cloudy. This blocks out the sunlight that corals and algae need to survive. People must remember that their actions on land affect life in the GBR.

THE GLOBAL THREAT

Now, Australia's creatures face a more serious threat. This threat affects reefs around the world. It also affects polar regions, deserts, and rain forests. This threat is climate change. The earth is gradually getting warmer.

Climate change is not new. The earth's climate has changed in the past. But today, change is happening much faster than before.

Global warming may be caused partly by human activity, such as air pollution. Cars and businesses release a gas called carbon dioxide into the air. When this gas enters the atmosphere, it traps heat from the sun. So, land and water temperatures rise.

It takes many years for animals and plants to adapt to change. If they cannot do this fast enough, they may die. So, global warming threatens life in the Great Barrier Reef and beyond.

The Great Barrier Reef's ecosystem is very delicate. The fate of one species can affect many others.

In the GBR, climate change causes several problems. The ocean absorbs carbon dioxide, which changes conditions in the water. Then, coral polyps are unable to form skeletons.

Another problem is rising sea levels. As glaciers melt, the water flows into the sea. In recent years, Australia's waters have risen slowly. Yet, most corals cannot survive in water deeper than 100 feet (30 m). If the ocean becomes deeper than this, the sun will not reach the algae. Then, the corals will die.

LIFE OF A CORAL

Healthy Coral zooxanthellae are living in coral tissue	**Bleached Coral** zooxanthellae are released from tissue	**Dead Coral** coral skeleton is covered in slimy, threadlike algae

coral

zooxanthellae   coral polyps

Corals are also sensitive to changes in temperature. Water temperatures must be between 60 and 95 degrees Fahrenheit (16 and 35°C). If the ocean gets too warm, corals become **stressed**. Then, algae leave.

When this happens, the corals look white. This is called coral bleaching. If ocean conditions return to normal quickly, bleached corals can recover. Still, this may take years. If corals remain stressed, they will die.

In 1998 and 2002, temperature increases affected much of the GBR. On average, about 60 percent of the reef bleached. About 5 percent suffered severe damage.

PROTECTING THE REEF

Over the years, many people have realized Australia's reef is special. In 1922, the Great Barrier Reef Committee formed. It set out to promote research and protection of the area.

By 1972, the Australian Institute of Marine Science was founded. This group works to understand and protect the reef. Their research supports many industries that use the area.

Then in 1975, the Australian government took action. It formed the Great Barrier Reef Marine Park. It also established the Great Barrier Reef Marine Park Authority to monitor activities there. The government of Queensland manages the park authority.

To protect the future of the GBR, **UNESCO** officials made it a World Heritage site in 1981. The site includes almost 135,000 square miles (350,000 sq km). This makes it the largest World Heritage site.

Our Valuable World Heritage

Around the globe, UNESCO World Heritage sites represent important civilizations and natural places. Cultural sites include historic buildings, towns, and monuments as well as important archaeological sites. Natural sites contain rare species or natural marvels. Or, they provide important examples of Earth's natural processes. Mixed sites share both cultural and natural elements. World Heritage sites protect and promote these global treasures for future generations.

Today, many **conservation** programs help protect the GBR. For example, the BleachWatch program encourages visitors to report bleaching. This helps scientists study the effects of climate change.

For better protection, the GBR is divided into zones. Certain activities are allowed in specific areas. These include fishing, tourism, shipping, and research. Activities such as mining and oil drilling are not allowed anywhere.

In 2004, the Australian government introduced laws that created no-take zones. Nothing can be removed from these areas. Today, 33 percent of the GBR is protected this way.

The Great Barrier Reef Climate Change Action Plan promotes practices that reduce **stress** on the area. Australia's communities are working to limit global climate change. But, efforts from countries around the world are also needed.

Most sea turtle populations are at risk. Yet, six species can breed safely in the GBR's waters.

For many years, studying the GBR was difficult. People could not easily conduct research underwater. Scientists collected sea creatures and plants. Then, they studied them in laboratories. There was no way to learn how these organisms lived underwater.

Then in the 1940s, scuba diving was invented. For the first time, people could swim underwater for long periods. This gave scientists new opportunities. Before 1960, only about 50 scientists had visited the GBR. With scuba diving, real exploration could begin!

Today, scientists have many questions. They want to discover how fast the climate is changing. And, they want to know how species will adapt to change.

The Great Barrier Reef is the perfect classroom for studying global warming. That is because it is sensitive to this change. What scientists learn there helps us protect other ecosystems, too. Protecting this natural treasure today will help preserve it for the future.

conservation - the planned management of rivers, forests, and other natural resources in order to protect and preserve them.

environment - all the surroundings that affect the growth and well-being of a living thing.

habitat - a place where a living thing is naturally found.

stress - strain or pressure.

tentacle - a long, flexible structure that sticks out of an animal, usually around the head or the mouth. Tentacles are used for feeling or grasping.

UNESCO - United Nations Educational, Scientific, and Cultural Organization. A special office created by the United Nations in 1945. It aims to promote international cooperation in education, science, and culture.

SAYING IT

Aborigine - a-buh-RIHJ-nee
algae - AL-jee
anemone - uh-NEH-muh-nee
cormorant - KAWRM-ruhnt
dugong - DOO-gahng
polyp - PAH-luhp
Torres Strait - TAWR-uhs STRAYT
zooxanthellae - zoh-uh-zan-THEH-lee

WEB SITES

To learn more about the Great Barrier Reef, visit
ABDO Publishing Company online. Web sites about the Great Barrier Reef
are featured on our Book Links page. These links are routinely monitored
and updated to provide the most current information available.
www.abdopublishing.com

INDEX

A
Aborigines 10
algae 6, 19, 22, 23
Australia 4, 10, 18, 20, 22, 24, 26

B
birds 14

C
climate change 20, 22, 23, 26, 28, 29
conservation 5, 16, 24, 26, 29
coral bleaching 23, 26
corals 6, 8, 13, 14, 16, 18, 19, 22, 23
crabs 12

D
dolphins 12
dugongs 12, 14

E
explorers 10

F
fish 12, 18

G
giant clams 12
Great Barrier Reef Expedition 10
Great Barrier Reef Marine Park 24
Great Barrier Reef Marine Park Authority 24

H
history 8, 10, 16, 23, 24, 26, 28

I
islands 4, 14

L
location 4

M
mangrove trees 14

O
octopuses 12

P
Pacific Ocean 4

R
reef formation 6, 8, 10, 14
reef structure 4, 6, 8, 14

S
scientists 10, 26, 28, 29
sea grass 14
sea snakes 12
sea turtles 14
shrimps 12
size 4, 5, 6
sponges 12
squid 12
starfish 12, 13

T
threats 13, 16, 18, 19, 20, 22, 23, 26
Torres Strait 4
tourists 16, 26

U
UNESCO 5, 24

W
whales 12